Let them asphyxiate with candy colored throes -

of spasms and flailing(s) and arboreal woes.

No mouths to shout out, no breaking the fall,

and swathes of Nature's nihilism devour them all.

Prepubescent feet trample bodies, aghast,

whilst disfigured survivors writhe, dying, en masse.

A herald for gloom when all's said and done,

Who could have known that death was this fun?

We'll tremble and shudder with seasonal lust.

All hail the reign of the almighty, the beautiful,

the Autumnal Rust.

Failure in 4 Parts

Part I: Grind

A storm is brewing small thunder-rumbles in the kitchen.

Coffee clears his head and the smell from the room.

Her arm jerks, an afterthought in oblivion, as he wipes the cooled sweat from her neck, sucking the salt from his fingertip.

God smiles outside the window-

Teeth like shards of yellow stained glass.

Part II: Weak

A swarm of locusts-drunken voices that devour thought with slur and swagger.

Dim light falls on pallid faces.

He watches from the corner as cold, damp hands grope exposed skin.

The ice shifts.

From the bar Typhoid Mary shoots shotgun blasts from her eyes.

As easy as he breathes, he dies.

Part III: Oblivion

The drive is long but the needle-pricks of rain on his cheek keep him awake –

aware.

It tingles like a sleepy limb.

She sits in the back so quiet and reserved –

when they arrive she slumps to the seat.

No one.

No body.

No thing.

A vacant house, gutted like a pumpkin, stares with vacant eyes.

He helps her to the edge, coaxes her to fly, and she leaps into the heavens.

For an instant it is beautiful.

For a second she ascends.

Icarus, unaware of failure, plummets to the gnashing maw below-

swallowed while smiling.

Part IV: Pain

An unwanted cigarette burns down to the flesh.

He crushes his fist, relishing the feeling before it fades, then drops it to a grave made of mud.

Extinguished, memory still throbs.

The Arsonist

Fire burns upon the horizon,

Haunting Stygian skies with flickering fingers.

It speaks in tongues, crackling and crashing in a chaotic cadence.

There is beauty in its rage.

Flesh and bone - wood and steel.

Unconstrained consumption.

No prejudice or preference to hinder the hunger.

Devouring both memory and dream,

An inferno of fury desires ALL.

Immortal. Perpetual. Incessant.

Death is the lifeblood and ash its legacy.

Why I Hate Winter

Oh how it slinks,

Prancing along on frigid tippy toes.

An ache permeates the marrow.

A hand upon the bones to still the steady rhythms.

It seems to outnumber the days -

long in tooth and unyielding in intent.

We pray for the thaw as it outstays its welcome.

Resting in our homes.

A numbing grue to further feed the oppression.

Lethargic -

we slumber.

Inevitable, the brumal cycle repeats,

And the beast simply sleeps and stirs,

Awaiting to awaken with an icicle smile -

arms spread across oblivion.

A Simple Truth

I'm a method actor.

All for nothing. Love and Hate.

The writer's lament.

So I light that smoke and choke down coffee to taste the disease.

Self medication is reality.

The jitters mean it's working, right?

My dog takes a shit while he eats more shit.

Is there anything more honest?

I bet he feels the tug of the inevitable at his soul.

The ache to be a real boy.

As do I. As do I.

Home Has a Face

My therapist asked me to think of my safe space.

My home.

When I think of a calm within the dark, where would I be?

She caught my hesitation and mistook it for a blank.

She was wrong.

It was you.

Limbs woven and cool sweat.

My lips against your neck and your fingers delicate spiders across my scalp.

I was already there before the words struck the space between us.

It was always you.

So I told her it was the ocean and the infinite space of waves,

Of cool toe tracings and the sound of white noise tides.

When all I could ever hear was the sound of your voice,

And the way you were always there, even when I didn't know your name.

Don't Use Dangerous Doors

There are places across the twilight,

Thresholds and gateways that weren't meant to be opened.

But if life is so short and humans so meek,

Why don't we?

Walk through, I mean.

Inebriate ourselves in lust,

Swollen and throbbing,

Stumbling into chaos.

Because death?

That bitch is the traveling salesman we all hate,

But,

She's already knocking on all of our doors.

Soft. Loud. Tempting. Terrible.

Purpose is perspective.

Life is the lock.

Devour Me

Let's peel off our skins again.

Rub against the wicked warm,

Sink our fingers into the form

Of being and life suspended,

An ache against the norm.

Can you imagine staying here forever?

The parting and breathless waves of pulses and shudders.

The heat in between the passing of time.

We will crawl into our bones and push into the waves,

Gasping to find the break,

Praying it never comes.

But when it does,

Oh how it does,

It crashes down with the weight of a thousand wanton moans.

Nothing More

So dark and deep is your ocean,

Sinking in the murk of life's endless drone,

All your sadness and sorrows they kill you,

Whenever you feel the most alone.

But I'd dive right into your waters,

Weightless, beside you, unknown,

To forever forsake the warmth of the sunlight,

And give you the breath from my lungs.

Intrusive Thoughts

He drives to work and thinks of how easy it would be to swerve into oncoming traffic.

Not because he wants to, but because he can.

Or how easy it would be to punch someone in the mouth simply for the sound,

Of knuckles hitting bone.

Teeth cutting away at restraint.

Are we wired for self preservation, or have we learned to be ashamed?

Life is an existential crisis,

With everyone to blame.

Clock in.

Clock out.

Masterbate.

Repeat.

Why can't we all be drunk and dumb and numb and hateful?

Civility is the real madness,

As we all claw at each other's throats

In silent reverie of the lives we already lost.

It's too bad our voices are balled and gagged,

I'd really prefer to hear about your rage.

Cowards.

Use the Fucking Phone

Okay, exaggerative stranger,

In your incessant ramblings with your old friend Susanne,

I'm trying to find Greek yogurt,

And you've taken an absurd stand.

In the middle of the aisle in whatever damn store,

What do you even think,

A fucking phone is for?

I don't want to hear about your hemorrhoids,

Or how loud your husband snores.

It doesn't matter what you're saying,

I seriously can't take anymore.

I want to ram my cart into your dumb legs,

Watch you crash and knock over a sales display.

But instead I'll kindly smile, and with a polite voice I'll say -

Excuse me, please (*would you use a fucking phone next time?*).

And go about my way.

Awake

Behind the veil of sleep I saw the red owl hunt.

White and crimson all over - aglow in midday rays.

I was afraid it would leave,

Terrible and magnificent.

I chased it from window to window.

Until I realized that it was there the whole time.

Tightly perched upon the corpse of a tree,

It stared at my face pressed upon the glass.

And as I looked it in the eye,

Through my own reflection,

The owl never wavered.

So neither did I.

Mother Nature's Duct Tape

Although my hands ache from the chill,

And I would trade my soul for anything but winter,

(demons inquire within)

There's just something about a new snow that makes it all better.

The world holds it breathe.

Do we have to go work?

Will there be school?

Is it safe to drive?

Who gives a fuck?

Snowflakes spatter on the tin roof and it's the only sound I can hear.

A cascade of white, suffocating in serenity.

Muffling the cacophonous clutter of complacency.

Just. Quiet.

A stillness that murders the monotony.

I'd applaud the show but that would make me a contradiction.

So I'll sit. Still. See if I can meditate enough to become one with my porch,

Think on nothing and the sublimity of solitude.

What would a porch think about?

Solidarity.

The Foundation is Fucked

If we're all a product of our environment,

What happens when we scrape off the layers?

How much of us is left when the pieces fall away?

A shivering, skinless facsimile of a persona,

Struggling to grasp at anything to fill in the gaps.

A fish suffocating to stay alive.

Death throes for amnesiacs.

Maybe we've placed too much stock on who we are,

Never appreciating where we've been.

Remembering how to breathe instead of forgetting how to exist.

The world will survive without us,

Time grinds long after we're rot.

Our place is nothing if not trivial.

Everything is nothing,

And it means the world to us.

Whispers of Ghosts We Forgot

Remember the moments of magic,

Times when youth made the world seem wondrous each day.

Friends who explored the universe and invited you along.

The grass between your toes,

Sweat and itchy skin.

There were monsters within the shadows,

Trees to scale and claim.

Screaming and squealing,

Laughter that wrenched the stomach tight in carefree bliss.

This should haunt you in waking,

Stalk your steps throughout the day.

The loyalest of any bonds,

You tried to lock away.

The Incorrigible Ache

Abominable, abhorrent son of a bitch.

Even when things are right it curls around your throat,

Takes its time to tighten the noose.

In flashes of memories and moments of desire.

It's the gift that keeps on giving.

A cold bed with a chalk outline where you used to sleep.

Arms that stretch for miles,

And fingertips that swell from the strain.

Whispering sweet nothings as it stabs you in the back,

The Ache revels in wretched release.

If doubt is the seed that spreads from absence,

Then there's nothing left but memory.

Sickle sharp and blood drunk.

Have You Ever?

Laid in bed for days like a boat lost at sea?

The blankets, waves,

awash in emptiness,

A world swirling around space as time arrests.

Eat when you remember.

Self care is a long nap that never ends.

An amalgam of nameless emotions pawing at your skin,

Melancholy moments for the weak of heart.

Dehydrated.

Alone.

Heavy as the heaviest thing?

No?

Me either…

What It Means to Dance

Take my hand.

Let's dance through moonlit shards,

Keeping steps to the silence of our songs.

Hold me tight and I'll guide you home,

Twirling beneath tired stars that burn in our wake,

A ball for the broken and buried.

If I stumble, you lead,

As I quicken the pace.

Your skin the color of sex,

And lips carved from the stories etched in your skin.

Let's show them what it's like to fall in step for the first time.

We are the curtain and the call.

The Very Bad Thing

Lumbering through the trees, stretching skin across bones,

The Very Bad Thing never ever slows.

A thunderous step, in poisonous wake,

Scouring for wandering souls to take.

Its mouth gapes open, its teeth ethereal,

Tendrils and talons of murderous material.

The roamers, the moaners, the lost ghost screamers,

It slurps up the essence of all in-betweeners.

Trapped in between alive and transcended,

The Very Bad Thing can smell life that's ended.

Hope that you're worthy,

Pay all your costs,

Or else you'll be snuffed,

By the devourer of the lost.

Make It So

Place it upon the wind with a tender touch,

Everything that stays buried will live in eternal ire.

Root out and nurture.

Eyelids stretch to scan the horizons.

Hope springs infernal.

Primal

I stopped wearing underwear today,

To tap into my inner animal.

Engorged with incessant hunger.

Held back by civility,

A limited libido buried by familiarity.

I want to be dangerous.

Teeth and flesh and tongue and bone.

Howl at the moon and retake the throne.

I used to be virile.

I'd growl and sharpen my claws.

Now I'm a middle-aged writer,

Waiting to rip away the facade I've claimed.

To bare the blood I chose to forsake.

And loose the beast unto your fields,

Craving to drink from your rivers,

And eat from the bounty of your skin.

Made in the USA
Columbia, SC
05 April 2023

14441246R00015